RESPECT

COMMIT

CHANGE

RESPECT

COMMIT

CHANGE

Facing The Truth and The Light

Herman O. Cooper Jr.

ARPress
ILLUMINATING IDEAS
EMPOWERING VOICES

ARPress
45 Dan Road Suite 5
Canton MA 02021

| Hotline: | 1(888) 821-0229 |
| Fax: | 1(508) 545-7580 |

Ordering Information:

Quantity sales. Special discounts are available on quantity purchases by corporations, associations, and others. For details, contact the publisher at the address above.

Printed in the United States of America.

ISBN-13:	Paperback	979-8-89356-640-6
	eBook	979-8-89356-642-0
	Harback	979-8-89356-641-3

Library of Congress Control Number: 2024903446

Table of Contents

DEDICATION

I dedicate this book to my family, friends, so-called friends, both men and women. Also to those physically and mentally challenged persons who are very special to me whom I had the privilege to work with for many years. Finally, all the other people with both positive and negative attitudes that made it responsible for making me open my eyes and mind to face the truth. The truth is I had to respect and accept "Jesus Christ as my Lord and Savior" and commit to praying if I wanted to change. Thanks to all of you for being a part of my life.

INTRODUCTION

The purpose of writing this book is to communicate to all people that RESPECT is one of the most important keys to life. There are things we have to do in order to gain and keep respect for an ongoing life requirement or need. I trust that it will enlighten the insight of many who have or are struggling to succeed. When God wakes you up in the morning, every choice after that is yours. How are you living? How are you thinking? If you're not thinking right, you're not living right.

OBJECTIVES

1. To reach out and encourage parents to love and respect their children and their children's friends.

    a. Help parents to evaluate their lifestyle to see if a change is needed.

    b. Help to empower parents to make the necessary change.

2. To reach out and encourage youth and young adults to show love and respect to all people.

    a. Teach them how to love themselves and to build their self- esteem.

    b. Teach them the positive aspect of being patient,

    c. Teach them the importance of self-control and,

    d. Teach them the value of life.

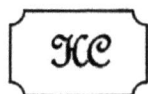

Chapter 1
SHORT LIFE STORY

Being in the world was fun, thinking it was all about me. All I cared about was what I thought was mine, not realizing that nothing was really mine, just the thought. It took me many years, lots of money, relationships, things, and many ups and downs to realize that everything that I had and everything I got belonged to God. He allowed me to use them.

I've come to realize that my journey through life, from childhood to manhood and from following Satan to following Christ is a journey we all have to take. In order for us to grow physically, mentally, and spiritually, this journey is a requirement. Looking back over my life, there were several people, places, things (money and cars), and words that had a real special and effective meaningful role in growing into manhood.

I am the oldest of ten children. In elementary school, we were taught to respect our parents, elders, people, places, and things in general. My father was very strict with my brothers, sisters, and me. We thought he was one of the meanest people in the world. It wasn't until years later we realized he was giving us tough love. My father worked nights, and before he arrived home in the morning, my mother had to be at work.

This was me (on the right side) before God changed my life.

My mother worked three blocks from the house, but some mornings, I had to walk to her job to get food for breakfast before going to school. Going to church several times a week with my other brothers and sisters will never be forgotten. There was a house on the corner and the first floor was converted into a church. The second and third floors were apartments and the basement was the grocery store. The garage was the area where we prepared pies and sandwiches to sell in the store or to be delivered to different locations and workers. We went to church on Wednesday evenings and Sunday mornings. Sunday evenings, we attended another church where a friend of our pastor was the preacher. They were like family churches, even though their names are difficult to remember.

My father believed that education was important. He made sure we understood therefore we had to study. When he was home, he would ask each of us, "What did you learn today in school?" "Do you have any homework?" "Have you completed it?" If the answer was yes, we then stood like soldiers to answer questions pertaining to our homework. The first time you hesitated or stuttered, he indicated that you didn't know your homework or you didn't learn the lessons taught in school. Homework or the lessons were returned to us leaving us to stand in the comer to repeat, answering the questions until we were able to answer every question asked. We would be up until midnight sometimes and still had to get up for school. Between nine and ten years of age, I started working for the pastor of our church and her husband. I worked in the store several evenings during the week, cleaning, scrubbing floors, bins, and stocking shelves. On Friday evenings I helped peel apples, peaches, sweet potatoes for pies and help make sandwiches such as fish, cold cuts, hamburgers, and other kinds of sandwiches. The garage in the back of the house had a wood potbelly stove, which was used to prepare the lunches to sell. We would get up early to finish preparing the lunches that were not finished the night before. We were out and on the road by nine o'clock. We would go to any place people were working, especially saw mills, construction sites, junk yards, to sell the foods.

We lived in the inner city at this time, and the peer pressure and distractions were tough. In the midst of everything, we were taught respect. There were consequences for your behavior, whether they were good or bad. I was also taught work ethics. I was taught time was money; you cleaned up what you messed up and you paid for anything you broke. Even though being careful in what we did was very important, education was still a priority. My father taught us how to fix and repair things, such as washers in the sink, clean and wax floors, how to cook, the proper way to set up to paint, and other things to do inside and outside of the house. He lived by statements like "Nobody wants a burden, not even your family." "If you don't have anything, you can't do anything, and if you don't know anything, you are a burden."

At the age of twelve, we moved from the inner city 1300 block of Division Street to the suburbs. I was able to attend Booker T. Washington School #130, which was still in the city and Sister Allen Family's church for a short time. In that transition from childhood to adolescence, I began misbehaving; however, the neighborhood children and adults looked out for one another. The neighbors were allowed to correct you in any way they thought was necessary. We thought at times our parents and neighbors were mean, but it was what they called tough love. It's not like that anymore. The parents do not want you to say anything to their children. The state will accuse you of child abuse.

My journey from a young male to a young adult became more intense. I was trying to stay on track with education because my father and mother demanded me. I was in the school band and was one of the best in the state, playing the clarinet for two years. Hanging out with the guys much older than me without my parents knowing taught me how to do anything and everything that I could do without getting caught. I got away with drinking, drugging, and stealing for a long time.

Due to this behavior, I was charged with statutory rape and went to jail for about three months. Because we both were still under the age of eighteen, the verdict was probation before verdict; meaning if I didn't get into trouble within that year, the charges would be dropped from my record. I had just graduated from Baltimore City College High School and ended up going to Baltimore City Jail. Hanging with the big boys on Pennsylvania Avenue, who were dealing in drugs, number running, and stealing gave me the impression that I was slick; still drinking, drugging, working and having fun. Church was not my priority at this time; drugs were out of control. I faced two options of going to jail or going into the service. I joined the Navy.

There is a list of names circulating around to show young people the approximate amount of jail time that the list of men had served. Wasted time, but thanks to God that most of the men, if still alive, have turned their life around and are trying to help the youth and giving back to the community in every effort. My nick or street name was on that list which was Boo.

I joined the Navy because I didn't want to run through jungles, farmlands, or anywhere that I would get muddy or dirty. I wanted to see the world. Seeing part of the world, I learned a lot about the culture of people as I traveled. My naval training began at a radio school in Bainbridge, Maryland. Fifteen students of different races were in my class. We got along just fine, but one evening after class, several of us went into the city to a restaurant and bar. There was one black man (myself) with four white men and one Puerto Rican. They ordered food and drinks and asked me what I wanted. I told them to order the same thing they ordered. The waiter taking orders refused to serve me, which discouraged me, so I left. The men asked the waiter why he did not serve me. He told them, we don't serve blacks.

They became very upset and told the server, if you didn't serve me, they were going to tear the place up. I told them it wasn't worth getting into trouble over a meal, so we left. Racism was then introduced to me.

I learned to read weather clouds, Morse code, signaling with my hands, lights, flags and also how to navigate ships. I was stationed on the LST Wood County 1178, which was a troop and weapons carrier. My life experiences on that ship were like no other, because there was some racism, but also respect and unity. You learned to respect the ranks of officers, if not the person themselves, and you learned what to say, when, where and how. You also learned about yourself and others, if you just watched and listened.

On the ship, you were allowed to carry a dagger to assist you in cutting open boxes or to complete other tasks that required a knife. There was a boatswain mate that would use his dagger in an attempt to intimidate crew members. He would cut them just enough to bleed a little. When he was angry, this type of action would put fear in you. No one that I knew ever told on him. Several men including myself fought him. In his case, he was feared more than respected.

My chance again to experience racism was with my E4 white petty officer. One evening, the ship received orders to evacuate people from the island of the Dominican Republic. The orders relayed to the crew were that there was to be a quiet ship and everyone would be up at zero six hundred, six o'clock. I was already on watch eight to twelve. So I sent word to my reliefs that I would stay on watch until two A. M., so I could sleep until six. I was relieved at two, and at four, my petty officers awakened me and told me that it was my turn to be on watch. I tried to explain to him that it was his turn to be on watch.

We argued for a moment, and then he moved his hand upward (standing in front of me) as to hit me. I hit him first, sounding off the General Alarm system on the ship, causing a lot of chaos, only to realize or to find out he was reaching for a cigarette in his shirt pocket. Because he was my superior officer, I was in trouble, so I had to call the Executive Officer and explain to him what had happened and why. He was upset, but he took care of the situation.

An incident happened to a crew member and what he did shows that people really don't know how stressful some people are and what they would do and the effect it has on you when watching things happen. You think about what the outcome will be or what could happen. We were on a training section in the Caribbean waters, when one of the crew members, who was going through loneliness, homesickness, etc., jumped off the ship into the water and started swimming around like he didn't have a care in the world. The alarm was sounded for "man overboard," and a boat was lowered to pick him up, with crew members wondering what if he drowned or what if sharks were going to attack him. He was removed from the ship and taken to the hospital for evaluation.

The most traumatic experience I had and even now forty years later, I am still affected by it. On the ship in the waters of Cape Hatteras, North Carolina, something was wrong with the anchor. We put a small boat over the side to see what was going on. We released the small boat from the hoist, when the wind and movement of the boat had the hoist swinging. In a quick second, the hoist hit the shipmate in the boat with me in the forehead and knocked him the same length of the boat which is approximately fifteen feet. His forehead was burst and bleeding, a couple of teeth broken, eyes blackened, and unconscious. Thinking he was dead, I began screaming and waving for help. It was when shipmates lowered a stretcher and climbed down to help, when I felt this hand on my shoulder. He was asking for help. It scared me out of my wits. To this day, I am always looking over my shoulder when I hear any movement, always a little nervous. I could go on, but they were my most heartfelt war stories.

Thanks to our neighbor, a Caucasian, my father, mother, and the Navy as they taught me how to dress and always be presentable because you never know what may happen in the course of a day. You could be offered a job, you may have to go somewhere your appearance may be looked at, or you may need to be taken to the hospital and you would like to at least look clean. I did buy a lot of nice clothes, and I still do when I can afford them. The first several months after being released from active duty, I didn't do anything but hang out with my friends all day and sometimes all night. I really felt grown, knew everything, wasn't ready to commit to doing anything, and couldn't get any real sleep. I didn't realize I was grown in age only and not the mind. A few months went past and my father instructed me to get a job to help around the house if I were going to stay there. He suggested and assisted me in getting a government job because it was more secured than most with secure benefits.

I applied for government jobs, took tests, and told it would be a few months before I would know the results. Later, I was hired at Armco Steel for a few months before being laid off. Working there, I learned how to be humble and do what was required because of safety hazards. I serviced the furnaces, janitorial work, and learned how to operate the overhead cranes. With the knowledge from Armco Steel, I was hired at Bethlem Steel and worked there for a few months until I was laid off again.

I was finally hired by the government as a card punch operator, but I wasn't making any real money, not knowing that in the near future, if I remain as an employee, there were more raises. I didn't stay for a couple reasons. I wasn't making a lot of money, I was living above my means, and I had too many women in one place. Unable to stay focused and unable to concentrate on work and partying too, I quit. I realized that I am not a person that can sit behind a desk all day, I had to be moving around and using my hands, so I was able to get a job at a steel mill, a subsidiary of Bethlem Steel, a plant called Buffalo Tank. I worked at Buffalo Tank for twenty-three years. I worked as office clerk, sales clerk, purchasing clerk, small truck driver, delivery person, shop clerk, assistant foreman, foreman, inspector, and when every supervisor would go on a staff meeting for a day, I would be the acting superintendent. I was the only black foreman at the Baltimore Plant. Buffalo Tank was a plant that built oil tanks, gas tanks, storage tanks, nuclear tanks, garbage stacks, and smoke stacks for underground and on top of the ground.

Later and even until this day, I thank God for giving me the opportunity to work there because of the valuable lessons I learned and were confirmed from lessons learned earlier. The lessons learned were for living your life. The first lesson was how to listen, understand, and follow before you can lead. The second was in order to build, you have to make plans, know what you want, what you need, order it, build and inspect it to be sure that it's what it's supposed to be. Third is, can a person change from being prejudiced to helping you willingly? These were things that I had one time or another, read in the Bible, and not knowing how they would show up in life later.

Going through my journey, I married three times, and every marriage was different. I am still in my third marriage because I had to look at myself and see what I was doing wrong. In the first and second marriage, I could place a lot of the fault on myself. I loved and lusted, but not equally, and in not doing that, I became selfish, not trusting, and most of all, no communication. In anything you do, especially in any relationship, you need that trust and communication. In going through those two marriages, there were a lot of ups and downs, heartaches and pain, and crying on my part. In the marriages, there were seven children involved, five boys and two girls. The boys' ages ranged from 11 to 20 and the girls' were 15 and 16. In the failure of the marriages, one son was incarcerated at the age of 24 and served fifteen years, one was murdered at the age of seventeen, and the girls struggled with men that weren't pleasing with us. You can see in relationships the things you have to do to keep good ones going. If they don't work out, they will affect everyone involved in some kind of way. Marriage is a great bond if you are ready and willing to put the time and requirements into it. It takes work, lots of work, and most of all, love. Love can conquer all, if it's real love, the love of God.

I felt stressed, anxious on and off the job for years. I always felt in a hurry or I had to rush, nervous, and I couldn't sleep or get any rest. I couldn't figure out what was going on with me so I thought drinking and drugging more would help; it did until it wore off. The spring and fall seasons were my worst months because the blowing of the wind and the bouncing of leaves on the ground enhanced my imagination of someone following me or was behind me. It had me jumping and turning around with my hands up in a defensive stand. My friends or people walking behind me would wonder what's up and at times were afraid also. In growing up, boys were taught, in order to be a man you had to be strong, endure pain, tension, stress, and have pride in yourself and that's what the most of us encountered. We didn't complain; we sucked it up and took the bitter with the sweet. I now take medication for some the conditions, but what worked best is the fact that I had the faith in God. I knew He would work it out for me because no matter what, He was in charge. I know "prayer changes things." I have gone to God in spirit and truth. He knows my heart; He knows my thoughts aren't always His and my actions aren't always His actions, but I am not out to hurt anyone and have asked for His help, guidance, wisdom, and understanding.

God had done great things for others. He has done great things for me, and will do for you if you just ask and believe. What I have asked for, He has given me in the words of God. I was instructed by the Lord to share with others. I want you to understand that things just don't turn good overnight, if anything, it gets harder at first. You have to realize that you are fighting the forces between God and the devil; you are fighting yourself to do good or bad. You will soon realize that in this world, everything is what you do or don't. It's for sure whatever it is you are doing or not doing, whether it is maybe or the in between, is the fact that you decide to do whatever you have on your mind to do; it's your decision. God gives us all a mind to use in order to make our own decisions. It takes some of us a longer time to commit to God's ways because of some sins and bad choices we made. We enjoy these pleasures until we or someone gets hurt. It took me years of searching, praying, and asking God for help before my life was turned around. It took so long because I wasn't ready to commit or surrender, to focus, or have the faith that I should have because I was looking for something that I felt, was supposed to be, but I found out not so. I first had to have a relationship with God and realize that my time is not His time. I had to realize that He is always in charge, no matter what a situation may be, and we may not understand or like the outcome. If you think about it, the only time things bother you are when you want it or want to have your way. If you didn't desire it enough or your way, you wouldn't care what happened. God gives you that peace that helps you understand if it's meant for you. You will get it, but if not, don't worry or become frustrated. I use to become frustrated. When I finally joined church, changed my life around, and tried to do the right things, they weren't given to me as I wanted them or the way I thought they were supposed to be in church. I was impatient. I read that just one of his days is a thousand of our years in the sight of God. I had to come to the realization God is in charge. I don't know where I am in God's time, but I have to be patient and wait on Him. I have been blessed to live seventy-four years. I am in fairly good health and have a fairly good life with ups and downs. I know as long as I live there are going to be more ups and downs, but I know God is in charge. He will see me through. He sent me a friend named Terry who gave me a book entitled God's Calling by A. J. Russell, which helped to start me on my way in changing my life. I want to do what God has assigned or asked me to do and that's to share with others or give back some of what He has given to me. He has given me life by showing me how to love everyone, have peace, understanding, and wisdom. There are nine words of wisdom God has given me to share with you what life is about and what they mean to me. They are Respect. Jesus. Faith. Communication. Praise. Temptation. Wisdom. Thanks and Blessed. You now have to look at them and choose what they mean to you. GOD BLESS YOU.

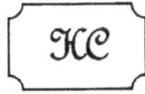

Chapter 2
RESPECT

Ready

Evaluate

Self

Pray

Expect

Change

Time

RESPECT

"high or special regard to something or someone, to consider deserving of high regard"

Respect is not given but something that is earned. Respect is an emotion that is in you and you use it as you feel. If a person speaks kindly to you or treats you nice, you give the same kindness or respect back, but if they speak negatively or in a mean attitude, then you would return in a negative or disrespectful way.

READY

"prepared for use or action, spontaneously prompt and willing, immediate available"

Ready is an action word that is one of the most important words that you may ever realize that controls your life. If you think about it, you would have to be ready to do anything whether you want to or not. If you have to get up in the morning to go to school, work during bad weather, or fulfill commitments, you have to be ready to roll with the punches. Being ready or getting ready isn't something that just happens. Depending on the situations, it is something that takes time, thought, and preparation. It can take minutes, for instance, getting up to go to work or school, take a shower, shave, dress, and eat, you usually place your mind on the order to do these things and the time it's going to take you to do them. Don't be late, which in most cases will take minutes. On the other hand, if you have an alcohol and drug problem, you know it could take years.

Again, ready is to realize the situation you may be in and how well you can adjust to being ready or not; just think that you are ready. As an example, you get up to go to work and have done everything you were supposed to do, got in your car and it doesn't start. You work on it for a little while and it still doesn't start. You become upset and call in to work to explain the situation, and you don't report to work. Your boss says he understands and will see you in the morning; things are fine. You were ready to go to work, but because of the situation you didn't go, but if you really wanted to go, you would have found another way of getting there.

Now in an alcohol or drug situation, you have to know that you are ready to stop using and clean up. There are so many obstacles in the way of the mind-set of addicts, because of the focusing and willpower they lack. They have to have the power of readiness to say no, and plant that thought, that my mind is made up and I am going to kick this habit, and do whatever it takes. You need to understand in situations like alcohol and drug cases that you may fail one or more times, but you have to focus on the fact that you are working hard on quitting. We also need to realize that we can't do anything or accomplish anything without God or your higher being. I hope you don't take the word "ready" lightly because it would be a big mistake; it's the first letter of the word respect.

EVALUATE

"appraise, put value on"

The second letter of the word respect is "evaluate." Evaluate doesn't mean that you become judgmental, but to be more investigative of yourself. You want to know about something, rather think you know about something. Evaluating will help you know whether or not you have thought about being ready or you know you are ready to take on a project. That is your decision. Evaluating is basically a self-worth issue. Knowing what and how you get what you want out of a project, you get involved. You decide how hard or easy it's going to be, how long it's going to take to accomplish your goal.

SELF

"the essential person distinct from all other persons in identity, and personal interest" is believing in you.

This is the biggest problem or toughest part of the word and meaning of the respect. We as humans allow three things to influence our minds and actions.

1. People: children's, wife, husband, boy, or girlfriend
2. Places: vacations, school, and work
3. Things: cars, drugs, houses, money, and jewelry

Once we have let one or more of these three influences control us, which we do often, we have allowed something else to control us, which isn't good because of the situations that we may be going through. Examples:

1. If your boyfriend or girlfriend makes you angry, you'll beat them up or worst is to kill them. How often have we heard, read, or seen in the news of this happening. A person was controlling the individual's mind.

2. When a place controls your mind, the same things happen there? We are afraid of losing a job or the job is too demanding, again we become upset and stressed, which causes an argument, threats, and occasionally murder.

3. If you allow things such as drugs or money to influence you, usually the outcome of these two things affects our community, families, and people. We know everyone needs money for one thing or another, but being on drugs, we demand more money. Really we will do anything to get it, whether it be borrowing, working, or stealing.

4. If we realize the outcome of letting something else control our minds, then we should know the importance of being more in control. We need to be real sure of who we are, where we are, and where we are going. If having God as our highest being, nothing else should control our mind even when it's very hard to do.

PRAY

"to ask earnestly for something, and to address God especially with supplication"

Praying is one of the most necessary parts and components of the word "respect." It's easy, just to ask God to help you, but the hardest part is trusting and believing He will. There are so many different religions and beliefs. You have to have your own relationship with God or your higher being, and know where you are in your relationship and belief in Him. Praying isn't something you do just to be doing it, it's something you want to do, and believing that something is going to happen. You should understand, no matter who or what you believe in, "it's only one God," no matter what you believe.

EXPECT

"looking forward to, waiting for something, or waiting for something to happen."

If you are reading this book, you are looking or wanting a change in your life. It comes a point in our lives, when we all get tired of rough times, angry people, confusion, or just the trials and tribulations we have to endure. When we get to that point in our lives, we want a real change, but don't realize how to accomplish it. If you follow these seven components and their meanings, there will be a change. The change may not be today, tomorrow or the next day, but believe, pray, and have patience; something special is going to happen. This process takes two very important avenues: "expecting something to happen, and having the faith that it will happen."

CHANGE

"to make or become different, replace with another, or exchange"

Change is the answer to your prayers or request that you've been seeking and hoping that it's what you desire. Nevertheless, it's something different. Now, there should be a change in you. Change comes in many forms and fashions, so be careful of what you ask for, because you just might get it. You should also realize that change may come in phases and not all at once. It may come a little at a time, and if that happens, then you will have to thank God anyway for what has changed and continue to expect more to come. The feeling you should have is waiting to have respect and give thanks for what has happened and for the things that are going to happen.

TIME

"a period during which an action, process, or condition exists or continues, or a point or period when something occurs."

Time is something that we should take very seriously, because the Bible says "there is a time for everything," no matter what it is. The only thing about this is the fact that you don't know how much time you have, whether it's a little or a lot. Time starts when you are born and stops when you die. Understanding that we know time is something we can't stop, so we should use it in our best interest. We can schedule time; however, there is some planning and thinking that has to be done to use it wisely. Know that even when you plan or schedule time, things happen, leading to some disappointments, whether they are cancellations, lateness, or just no shows. Dealing with kids, you have to be very careful, because they take things to heart and hurt easier than adults, even though that is questionable. Parents setting times, places, and events with the kids, set a feeling that you should know, because it's the same feeling you may have when your boyfriend, girlfriend, husband, or wife sets something up with you. The joy, happiness, and loving, feeling or thought, are something we all want to feel from our special people, and if nothing materializes, no call or no show, the feeling with men is hurt. It's hard at times to explain to kids what

happened, even explaining to adults, but as adults, we know time and things must go on.

We spend a lot time thinking negative, being angry, and just worrying about things in general. Some things we have control over and some things we don't. For example, we usually worry about things, but not necessary things we need. We desire a lot of money, designer clothes, and shoes, nice cars and homes, certain people to like us, a job that pays well, have good kids with the same thoughts when they grow up. We have learned, taught, and understood that everything we may want may not be good for us, and it takes time and work. Understand that there is nothing free, even the air you breathe, because if you don't breathe it, you don't receive it, so you have to put some effort or work into it. You should also realize that tomorrow is not promised to us, so do all you can today. I know we all know someone younger and older that have passed on and we know some people that are worse off than we are, so put yourself in their place for a moment and consider how they are feeling. The question probably is, "Why am I like this?" In your lifetime, you are going to have some good times and some bad times, so be encouraged and try to have more positive thoughts than negative. I am not saying it's going to be easy, because it's not, but when bad times come, look behind at the person that's worst off than you. Try to help someone at times. If you look at life as one great big circle, you all should understand that if each one helps one, then you will be one of the persons being helped at sometimes in your life. You need to know that you don't want to be the person in the center of the circle, because for a period of time, you will be receiving from everyone. When one realizes that you are doing all the receiving and not giving, everyone will stop and cut you off and now you

are all alone. That's not a feeling you want to have or a place you want to be. We know in everything or in some situations, people just don't listen or try. In reading this book, especially if you have kids, grandkids, friends, or relatives that are hard to reach, take the time and be responsible enough, along with patience, to teach them to use their time positively and wisely. The most important thing about time is that God's time is not our time, and He is in control. Again if you don't have what you desire, it may not be the time for you to have it, so wait on the Lord and be encouraged because what is meant for you, will be received in time.

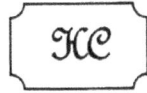

Chapter 3
JESUS

Jesus

Erase

Sins

Unbelievers

Surrender

JESUS

Definitions of Jesus from the Bible, Hebrew chapter 4 verse 14, and 1st John chapter 4 verse 15

Jesus, whom so ever, shall confess that Jesus is the son of God, God shall dwell in him and he will in God.

Jesus, son of God, great high priest

Jesus is my God and my reason for living. I am nothing without Him. I believe in Him for my every need, for help to get through trying times while on earth. I ask Him to help and teach me to be a better Christian, which consist of helping, forgiving, and sharing with your enemies and fellow man. "Thank You, Lord."

Jesus is my higher power. He is the son of my God and the reason for my being. Everything that I have and is to receive will come from Him. I believe that my God created all of heaven and earth and everything that is in it, so therefore everything belongs to Him. I know He gives us what He desires us to have according to His will. There are times we steal from God. It's a known fact that we didn't create these things, so you must believe. If you don't believe in my God, then who or what created you? Again my higher power is Jesus, the son of God. This portion of this book will reflect what He can and will do for you and me.

ERASE

"to rub or scratch out, cancel or delete"

There are times when we have done things and hurt people, even family members, and we were sorry what happened and hope that they would forgive and forget. There were times these persons forgave and forgot the things we had encountered, even though we were happy for the forgiveness. We felt guilty about those actions, but we wondered and asked the question "why?" It's because God has laid upon their hearts and souls to forgive. Jesus, being our guide, gave His life on the cross for us; therefore, our sins have been erased. We still sin daily by word what we say, thought, what we think, and deed, things we do. If He forgives us for the sins we commit, don't you think we can and should forgive those who commit sins. I know you have heard of the golden rule, "do unto others, as you would have others to do unto you," think about it. If you treat a person nice, don't you want to be treated the same, but it doesn't always happen that way, so feelings are hurt. If the truth be told, we, at times, curse at people, want bad things to happen to them, steal from them, scratch cars and flatten tires, but we wouldn't want for those things to happen to us. They are some of those words, thoughts, and deeds that come to mind but need to be erased.

SINS

"an offense against God, weakened state of human nature in which self- controls your thinking."

Sins are bad words, thoughts, and deeds previously discussed. Sin is an action that we allow to take over our minds, which causes us to react negatively; we need to erase or control. If we allow sin to control our minds, we will become losers and not conquerors. Our goal is to become conquers or overcomers.

UNBELIEVER

"doubter"

Being an unbeliever hinders you from having the confidence you need to achieve the things you desire/wish to accomplish in life. You may have doubt to achieve. I doubted my ability to write this book, because there were a lot of things going on in my life that were mind controlling, but I had to pray, seek my God, and knock on His door (spirit) and ask for patience, knowledge, wisdom, and belief that I could accomplish this goal. I also, asked for His purpose and it was to make a change and help His people understand that there is a division between His people and Him and no unity among His people. "Together we stand and divided we fall." If you don't believe in yourself or your higher being, you can't believe in anything positive. I believe in myself, my God that dwells within me and know that He will help me to endure any obstacles that try to hinder me from being a conquer or overcomer.

SURRENDER

"to yield to the power of another, or act of giving up or yielding oneself."

In many cases, when we hear or see the word "surrender," we think of being conquered, but not this time. You realize in order to become a conqueror, you need help, and what better helper than your Creator or higher being. I had to surrender my life to my God, in order to get a clear and peaceful awareness in my life in order to raise my children in the way they should grow. It did not work always perfectly in each of them. I did what I was supposed to do and left the rest to God. They now have minds of their own. They chose the paths they wanted to take; however, some came back and the others are working their way back with God's help and guidance. I give my God the praise and thanks that He taught me to realize that if there is something I want now and don't have it, that maybe it's not for me right now, but in His time. I thank Him that I don't crave for anything except to do His will. Our wants again hurt us. I consider now the importance of things, watch people pay $50 and $60 dollars for a pair of gloves, when that same amount of money will buy a pair of gloves, a scarf, and a jacket. People pay $150 to $200 for a pair of name brand tennis shoes when a pair of $40 tennis shoes would take them to the same place. It's the same thing with cars, homes, and clothes. I guess it's okay if you can afford it, but to go into a hole to impress someone else is surrendering and for the wrong reasons. You should accept who you are and not for what you have or can give.

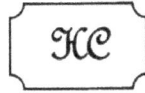

Chapter 4
FAITH

For

All

Individuals

To

Have

FAITH

"allegiance to duty or a person, belief and trust in God or complete trust." Faith is something that we all should have or it's referred to as hope.

"Faith is the substance hope for, but evidence of things not seen." In other words, you have to believe it's going to happen or come, but you don't know how or when it's going to come. It's belief or trust in God.

FOR

"a preparation toward or toward the purpose or goal of time."

In this case, faith is for you if you only believe in God. Again, "faith is the substance hope for, and the evidence of things not seen." If there is something you want or need, you have to pray and believe that you will receive it, even though you don't see or know how or when it's going to happen. The Bible states that "if you have the faith of a mustard seed," you can move mountains. You can, with belief and patience, which is very hard, because we don't believe in things we can't see, and we don't want to wait too long, we want things right now.

ALL

"the whole of, every member of, the whole number, quantity, amount or everybody."

"All" means everybody, every man, woman, and child. It includes every race, creed, and religion. The only thing that is required of everyone is that you believe. It would also be helpful to help one another to understand that they need a relationship with God or the higher power.

AN INDIVIDUAL

a single member of a category, or a particular person.

An "Individual" in this case is you. My Jesus wants you to have the "faith of a mustard seed to move mountains." Do you realize how small a mustard seed is? Being an individual, you need to know, your mountain or mountains may not or will not be the same as other people's mountains. Understand your mountain. A person building a road, their mountain would probably be a rock formation, but to you, your mountain may have been money that you didn't have to pay your bills or it may be having family problems with children, wife, husband, etc. Being this individual, my relationship with my higher power (JESUS) helped me to understand the more I hear or read about something, the more or less interested I am going to gain. When it comes to having faith, which is a gift my God gave me, I understand the importance of faith. We have to believe and have patience because we don't know how or when we will receive what is needed or desired.

TO

"a state of consciousness or awareness."

It's time to be aware that you must have faith, which is "the substance hope for, but the evidence of things not seen." Being the kind of people who need to see something in order to believe hinders us in the way that if it's not seen it's not real. It took me a long time to understand it, but with the help of my God and the people He put in my life, I realized that faith is necessary to have in order to make it through life. It was brought to my attention that you can't see air, but we are breathing it every moment we are living.

HAVE

"to hold in possession."

You now have the opportunity to possess the reality or know what it means to have faith. You can have faith in many things, including yourself, so be very careful of what you believe. Know that if you have the faith of a mustard seed, in God, your higher power, you will be covered in everything you need in your time.

HC

Chapter 5
COMMUNICATION

Communicate

Open

Mentors

Miracles

Unite

Nurture

Interact

Committed

Active

Tribulations

Invite

Overcomer

New

COMMUNICATION

"to make known or to pass from one to another"

Communication is very important in life because if we don't communicate, there are things we are going to miss, such as the lack of knowledge, understanding, obedience, wisdom, and forgiveness. We need communication to know who we are, whose we are, where we are going, how we are going, what we are going for, and how long it's going to take.

Communication is so important in everything you do, when dealing with people. In life, you will have to communicate with every living thing in some kind of way, even with yourself. Plants have to be watered, animals you talk to or train, and people we talk to and receive an understanding of how, what, and where things are to be done. You also have to communicate with yourself to make sure you breathe, eat, drink, and sleep. Supervisors teach their workers how to do what's needed for their job, parents have to teach and show their children about life and what is expected and is required of them to be productive. Children have to learn to listen and relate (talk) to parents or teachers to get their point across or to understand what is being relayed to them. It's hard at times to communicate to some people; it takes patience. It's hard for some people to understand the first contact, so it may take several encounters because of some physical or mental reason. At times, we may have to look at ourselves to make sure we are communicating in a proper manner. We want to be sure that a person is receiving information in the way we want them to in a way that it may be easier for them to receive. We need to be mindful of the way we talk to people and even animals. We may need to ask ourselves, "are we speaking too loud or too low, are we speaking clearly or are we calm or excited, and are we facing them or looking off?" If the answer is yes, then we need to make a change in the way we are transmitting the message; this is communication.

OPEN

"not shut or shut up, readily accessible or cooperative."

We have to be readily accessible and cooperative to receive positive or negative criticism. Let's face it, at times we aren't ready to except anything, much less negative criticism about ourselves. We always want to think we know best, have thought out our issues to the point that we are right, even though we may be wrong or not looking at better recourses. This type of communication is about us and how open we are to receive and our ability to pass on information to others for whatever reasons.

This book discusses the fact that there is not enough respect, love, or charity among people and the belief in JESUS or the higher power is falling short. My belief in my God is stronger, than some others' belief in a higher power. In reality, we didn't create heaven, earth, animals, or ourselves. Realizing that there is a creator, no matter what you call him, He's like a light switch, turn it on to open the circuit to get the electricity flowing. You have to open up your heart and mind to relate to others the goodness, mercy, and grace of the Creator. We should give respect and thanks for everything they have done for us. If we show our respect along with others, we can make a change in this world. JESUS is the truth and the light.

MENTORS

"trusted counselors or guides"

I am and hope you would like to be a trusted counselor or guide someone. We are a great source to different people such as a brother, sister, mother, father, wife, husband, friend, or a boss. Are we trusted mentors to these people under our care? Gangs are recruiting kids, college students, and even teachers to organize business like organizations, but are they the type of trusted counselors or guides we want in our society? If it is, then we are looking for trouble. There are some people that want to keep trouble and chaos in the world. It looks like fun, at times profitable. The sad thing is that you will realize that it doesn't last and it will not really make you happy. Those of us who have experienced this behavior realize that we have been spared and blessed to be able to become the trusted counselors and guides that may train or show others God's way to get happiness out of life. Granted, it may not be the fun or as profitable as you may like it, but it will be rewarding and a blessing to others. We are to please God and to help others, hoping that it will spread and show the world that if each one helps one, which becomes a circle of good will, it's going to make a change.

MIRACLES

"an extraordinary event manifesting divine intervention in human affairs, or an unusual event, thing or accomplishment."

You are a miracle at this moment; you are alive, reading, and hopefully understanding this book and what it means to everyone that is able to read it. Somewhere, there is someone that was here yesterday, but isn't here today. There are persons alive that don't have the full control or strength of their limbs or mind. Depending on how old you are, things have happened to you or someone you know. They may have survived a situation or someone else who couldn't handle the pressure and didn't make it. There are many things that we could consider miracles, but there is only one way, with God and your help, make things plain and help others understand that we all need to make positive choices in our lives. We can do this by letting people know that there is a God and by asking for help. He will give us the help we need to accomplish His will and for us to help others. Two of my miracles or testimonies are:

1. I have a nephew that was shot in the head, the bullet went around his skull and came out of the same hole; he was partially paralyzed for several months but has fully recovered.

2. I was in a car accident, where I hit a car and spun around hitting a tractor trailer and then a tow truck which crunched the car like a straw, causing me to have to be cut out of the car. My injuries were a broken left arm, several cracked ribs, cracked back, and broken collarbone. I was out of work for five months, but I had a gentleman to work for me in a machine

   shop running a drill press, and he sneezed, resulting in him having several surgeries and out of work for four years.

These incidents should show you that there are miracles being performed every day.

UNITE

"to put together so as to make one or join in interest or fellowship."

I'm hoping that this word "unite" will identify the true meaning, not the meaning of a gang of destruction, but with a group of people that are trying to make a positive change in the world, or our community. We have to understand an old saying, "together we stand and divided we fall"; it's the truth. When uniting, you have to be ready to become as one, and on the same accord, if you aren't ready to become as one, you become the weakest link or part of the group which will allow confusion or separation. This is something we need to explain and teach our children that it is important to communicate about issues on how people need to come together. I am hoping that we all come together in strengthening our families and stopping the violence. If we don't stand for something, we will fall for anything. There is strength in being united.

NURTURE

"training, to care for, or upbringing"

Nurture or nurturing is something we all need for ourselves and if we are capable, we should nurture to help others. If you are a parent, you should be nurturing your children in every way that you can, to ensure that they become great citizens, children of God, respectful, and maybe mentors. We all need guidance because it's so much evil doings in our world today. At times we get caught up in making the wrong decisions. We will sometime enjoy doing the wrong things, but that doesn't make it right. In telling the truth about the early parts of my life, I enjoyed doing the wrong things at times, not realizing that my God was watching over me. The things I did and thought I got away with, other people didn't get away with. These things I am sharing is to mentor or nurture my children or others. I thank my God for watching over and blessing me. I have survived and others have died or are serving long prison terms. I thank my God for His grace and mercy and opportunity to share my experiences with others. It's a known fact that you can't properly teach or tell someone about something if you haven't been there or done those things. Let this time be our opportunity to share your experiences or testimonies in order to nurture someone.

INTERACT

"mutual or reciprocal action or communication between persons."

To interact with others, sometimes is hard to do, but it's necessary that we learn to interact. We at times think we know it all, but I am letting you know we don't. There are times we don't trust the people that are trying to help us, but believe the individuals that encourage us in doing something wrong and seeming fun. There are times you have to believe half of what you see and not what you hear. Investigate situations for yourself. As an example, in a relationship, you maybe a person that loves to smile and hug, but your partner does not. They see you somewhere in the (mall or store) hugging someone. A friend reports that you are fooling around, but in reality, you are just hugging someone you haven't seen in a long time and just happened to run into them and enjoyed seeing them. There you are seen hugging someone and they are just a friend, and their friends have them believe that you are doing something wrong, but you are innocent. It does not only happen to us, but we do the same thing to others. If we pray and interact with the right people, we hopefully will not allow tricky to become a downfall in our lives. Be careful of how and who you try to interact with for what reason.

COMMITTED

"to put in charge, trust or pledge, or assign to some particular course or use."

Committed pertains to you and me. You will have to ask yourself if you are willing or what you are willing to be committed to. I have committed myself to writing this book hoping to make a change in the world and hoping that the people that read this book would be committed to doing the same, with the help of my God. Committing yourself hopefully means that you have prayed and thought and are ready to do whatever is necessary to help someone make a positive change or decision in their family, community, and the world. We want to be committed men, women, and children to God and His people according to His will.

ACTIVE

"causing or involving action or change and presently in operation or use."

Once stated "you can't show or tell someone about something if you haven't been there or done that." Communication, which is an action word, is about me and God in me. Once you read this, you may be able to add yourself in becoming active if I can't help you; I am not going to hinder you. In my younger years, I tried to do anything and everything I thought was big enough and bad enough to do. I was real active in things I thought was fun, but not always right. The older I became, in and out of trouble, my God helped me realize that He has been watching over me. I prayed and asked for help and He answered my prayers by helping and showing me a more Godly way instead of a worldly way of being active in my life. I wasn't involved with my family or other important things in my life as I should have been, but after praying and asking my God for help and guidance, He put people, places, and things in my life to help change things. He gave me the wisdom to know that I had a problem, an addiction and that I needed to conquer them both. My God prepared me to do both, face and conquer my problem (frustration) and addiction (drugs) by instilling in my spirit that I was READY to except the challenge and to do BATTLE.

I became more active in praying, going to church, being with my family, work habits, physically challenged people, and now I am a mentor for a young man in the Big Brother and Big Sister organization. Working with physical challenged people made me realize how blessed I am and have blessed most of us are, but didn't realize it. The physically challenged people except the way they are, and try to live a normal life, but we so called normal people are the ones that give them the most grief and discomfort; we are the ones that complain the most. They show more love and compassion than we do toward one another. I will tell anyone that I hear complaining about an issue, to look behind you and look at someone else that doesn't have what you have and thank God for what you have. We as parents really need to get real active in our families, because it does take two. We need a village to help us. Men can't teach a girl to become a woman, and a woman can't teach a boy to become a man, so somewhere along the line, a child needs a man and a woman in their life. I want to be a blessing in someone's life, so I am active, and hope if you are not, that you will become active.

TRIBULATION

"distress or suffering resulting from oppression or persecution, trying experience or affliction."

In life as long as we are living, we are going to have some tribulations, not just one but many, depending on how we handle them as long as we are live. It's very important to have a relationship with God. My God tells me, that I will have perfect peace if my mind stays on Him. He didn't say that I wouldn't have trials and tribulations, but I would have peace if I concentrate on Him. I find out that it's the truth. When my mind is concentrated on Him, I don't worry or think about any of my problems or issues. You will find out, the only time you hurt really bad is when you want something or want something to happen and it doesn't happen. Our wants hurt us more than anything else. Here are two examples that occurred in my life:

1. I wanted and bought a new car. I was living above my means. I wasn't listening and not making enough money to keep up the expense. The car was repossessed, causing me to owe money on something I didn't have, and leaving me with bad credit and without transportation to and from work or activities. A friend gave me an old car that needed brakes, grill, and other repairs. I had all the work done for less than

a car payment on a new car. The old car took me to the same places and cheaper than the new car.

2. Like other men, I wanted a woman because she was pretty, but not listening again or realizing that she may not be what I needed, but what I wanted. I wined, dined, and married. In years to follow, I gained a lot of debt, jealous of her fooling around and almost losing my freedom, because of what I was and wanted to do to her. I thank my God that I remembered what He said about wanting peace. I prayed, cried, and focused on what He had told me, and we were able to move on without any real life threating incidents. We did have some physical incidents, but thank God, no one had any serious injuries. The key to this concept is if I didn't want what I wanted and had listened to my God or the people He sent to me to watch and pray, I wouldn't have had such a hard time in those times. I look back on these incidents as testimonies in my life. Someone else, maybe going through now or in the future could look at this and be more aware of what to do. If you keep your mind focused on God, He will bring you through and see that you get what you need and not always what you want. What you want may not be good for you, such as drugs or gangs.

INVITE

"to request the presence or participation."

I hope that you have read and understood this testimonial because it makes the word "invite" simple. You should understand you have to invite God into your life and mean it in order to have a good and prosperous life. I don't know about your higher being, but my God will not just come into your life without being invited. My God wants to know that you want a relationship with Him. That's why He tells me, "seek ye first the kingdom of heaven, and all its righteousness and all things shall be added to it." My God wants me happy in Him first, but we want happiness in our own ways and right now; it may not be our time. We have to have patience so we can appreciate the good things that will come our way in our time. Our time is not God's time. We don't want to have to repeat an old saying: "easy come, easy go." Many of us have had to face the fact that we have to work for what we want in order to appreciate what we have and accomplished. My God will help you realize the fact, without a lot of pain and suffering, He shows us that we don't appreciate the things that are given to us as much as things we work or sweat for.

OVERCOMER

"means to conquer or make helpless."

The definition of this word defines what we desire to become. We, as humans and victims of this society and economy issues, are fearful. In our lifetime, we can be over a lot of things: overweight, overconfident, overexcited, and overloaded, but what we are looking for is to be overcomers or conquers. In order to be a real conquer, it goes back to the last word invite. Inviting Jesus into your life and letting him take control will help you become that conquer. The Bible states in Philippians chapter 4 verse 13, "that I can do all things through Christ which strengthen me." With that strength and your belief, you are a conqueror or an overcomer.

NEW

"recently discovered, different from former recognized or beginning."

You should feel great about yourself at this point, if you haven't before. This is the point we all are looking to explore. If you have invited God into your life, let Him guide, and have control of your life. You are an overcomer and you are a new individual. You realize that there is a change in you, maybe not a big change at first, but a change even if it's only in the way you are thinking. It's going to take time, but it's a new beginning and that's where we have to start. This new beginning consists of a new attitude, a new talk and a new walk. The new attitude is for each one to help one to get to this point and then help them to take one step at a time.

Chapter 6
PRAISE

Pray

Regularly

Always

Increasing

Self

Esteem

PRAISE

"to give approval or thanks to something or someone that has done something good or great for you."

We should give God or your higher power, all the praises, because He has done something that no one else could do, and that's give us life, not only life, but He gave His own life that we might live and live it abundantly.

PRAY

"Pray means to ask earnestly for something from God or your higher power."

When you pray, you should make it plain and simple, but most of all direct and sincere. Praying and having faith go hand in hand because once you have asked for something, you have to believe you will receive it in time. You again will have to have patience, because things don't always happen when we want it. God's time isn't our time, so you are going to have to wait, maybe a short time or it could be very long, but if you pray and have the faith of a mustard seed, it will come as long as it is God's will. You should also be careful of what you pray or ask God for. You just might get it, and sometimes it may not be what you need or really want. God wants and gives us good gifts, but we want what we want, whether it is good for us or not.

REGULARLY

"constant, often, arranged in accordance to rules or some kind of structure."

Praying and praising God is something that we should do every moment, much less every day. We should pray day and night because that's how we give God most of our praises, which means that our minds are stayed focused on Him. If we keep our minds steadfast on God, we are giving Him the praise and glory He so richly deserves. It helps to keep us in perfect peace and out of trouble. We all need to pray regularly, which is day and night, but to be truthful about it, we sometimes do not; that's why we aren't in perfect peace and we remain in trouble.

ALWAYS

"means all the time or forever."

We should always give praises and thanks to God because it's all about Him and not about us. We should understand that He is in charge whether we want Him to be or believe that He is or not. We are always going to have some ups and downs. At times, we are going to be in some situations that we will know was not a way we could have escaped without some help, not knowing where or how that help was coming; however, all of a sudden something or somebody shows up to rescue us, mainly from something we have done to ourselves. Here is an example of what my God can do to show you a miracle. You may use an alarm clock to get you up in the morning, but take that same alarm clock to the graveyard and see who gets up. This is something to think about as long as we live.

INCREASING

"to become greater, growth, or addition."

Life is a learning process, and during the course of living, we should be increasing several things. We should be increasing in at least three important things such as wisdom, knowledge, and understanding. Increasing our understanding indicates that life is something given to us by my God and we need a relationship with Him. Increasing our knowledge indicates that we understand and have a relationship knowing for ourselves that there are some things we have to do in order to live the life given to us (such as eat and drink). Increasing in wisdom indicates that we understand who we are and whose we are. We should have the knowledge of the things we have to do in order to live a productive and comfortable life; things such as working, getting a good education, and taking care of our body (God's house), mind, and soul.

SELF

"the particular person from all other persons in identity."

In the word praises, the letter S represents self, which is you or me. Self has a lot of words that can make or embarrass you. One word is self- assurance, which is a good one, but self-destruct isn't; however, no matter which word you use, it's you or me. When I speak of praise, it's giving thanks, glory, and honor to my God. We should give praises in bad and good times, because if we didn't have the bad, we wouldn't know the good, and if we didn't have the good, we wouldn't realize the bad times. In having the different times, we will realize in some of those times, we won't know what happened, but we will realize that it wasn't our doing.

ESTEEM

"to set high value on respect or admire."

Esteem is one of the words that you can add the word "self." Again esteem is a character of self and only we can control it with the help from our God. I found that if it wasn't for my God, which I give thanks and praises to, somebody, someplace or something would have taken control of my mind and stole my self-esteem. I will say for a period of time, something and somebody did steal my self-esteem and controlled my mind. My wife left and took my kids, and I turned to drugs. I allowed these two things to take control of my life for a time. I thank my God that He helped me to keep my mind stayed on Him to bring me back to my senses, and to understand that He is the only way to keep from allowing people, places, and things to control you.

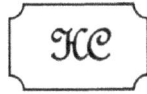

Chapter 7
TEMPTATIONS

Taking

Enemies

Meek

Plant

Thirst

Authority

Teach

Inheritance

Obey

Natural

Sufficient

TEMPTATION

"an action induced by people, places, or things to encourage you to do something whether it is right or wrong."

Temptation is a mind-controlling emotion; it causes your desire to take control of your actions.

TAKING

"to obtain, secure, choose for use to bring into relation."

Taking is an important word because it has several meanings, and it's a word that we need to understand. Out of all the meanings, it's certainly meaning that we need to absorb or use. It's like life, there are several things we do and things we want to do and also certain things we have to do. In life, we have to eat and drink, especially water, but we have to do something in order to get food and water, or we will surely die. In life, you will be making choices on what it is you want to do and how you are going to do it. One thing for sure, you will or should be taking responsibility for your decisions. In taking responsibility, you will have to choose the way you want to go, observe the pros and cons of the project or projects. You want to be confident and secure on what it is you want to do and bring it into existence to the best of your ability. I am not saying it is going to be easy, but if you are taking advantage of your main source which is God, then He will see you through and help you not to give up but to help you to be a conqueror, no matter how hard or how long it takes to finish the race or project you started.

ENEMIES

"one or more person or forces that attack or try to harm another."

Enemies come in many forms, women, men, money, and drugs, as some examples. I can't express enough the importance of one taking advantage of your source which is God, by praying, praising, and giving Him thanks for everything He has done and doing for us right now. If you just look and listen to the things that are going on around you, you may say that you are lucky, but we are blessed. We know there is a difference between good and bad, and so does the people that are committing the different deeds. We know that gangs and criminals are creating the problems as far as killings, robberies, rapes, etc., but in the last few years, the people who are supposed to protect us from the bad guys are committing the same crimes if not more than the real criminals. So "what are we to do or who do we look to?" The only thing we can do is pray for them all and our situations and believe that God will change things and know that He can and will. We still need to stand fast, pray, praise, and give thanks.

MEEK

"characterized by patience and long suffering/deficient in spirit of courage."

Meek is something that we all should be, but not considered as being wise as the definition stated. In life or should I say "street language," a meek person is considered as being a weak person, even though that's not true in all cases. Yes, in some cases a person that has low self-esteem, not sure of himself, and allows others to take advantage of him, are considered weak or meek, but this also could be fear. Once, you have confidence in yourself, know who you are, and whose you are, you will become a different person, because now you are meek, humble, and not fearful. The difference is that God has given us a conquering spirit and we realize that people are taking our kindness for a weakness; we can change that situation.

PLANT

"establish/ settle/ to place firmly or forcibly to set in ground to grow."

When we think of planting something, most of the time it's something going in the ground, but I'm hoping to plant with God's help, something positive in your heart and mind. I want to plant in your heart and mind that you are somebody and people are watching you. You may not know it, but you could be someone's mentor, and they could be watching to see you doing something positive or productive to encourage a healthy lifestyle. If you are doing something negative, it could have a negative effect on their life and how they feel about you. I hope, with my God, He can plant a positive plan or seed in your life to live by; you can be used to plant a plan or seed into someone else life and they can carry it on and on. That plan is called "each one helps one," and it will make a change in our homes, communities, cities, states, countries, and the world. We may never see it get that far, but we can see it get started. I never thought I would get to see a Black President, but thanks be to God I did, confirming that all things are possible if you only believe through Jesus Christ.

THIRST

"to have a strong desire or craving for."

When we think of "thirst," we crave for water or some other beverage. Please understand when I use the word thirsty, it's not always talking about a beverage. There is a thirst for a greater relationship with God. I trust that you are craving and thirsting for more knowledge of God. We can live the way He would have us to live, which is comfortable and happy. Knowing how we are supposed to live, we should crave or thirst for the knowledge of doing what we have to do to get to where we want to be. We may not physically drink the knowledge, but we surely have to believe, seek, read, and absorb the knowledge as we grow. We are nothing without Him.

AUTHORITY

"to influence thought or behavior or person in command."

I am glad that I let God have the authority over my life because He as the Creator; He knows what is best for me. The choices I made in the past and choices I have made lately have not been very good. Being human; some choices I will make in the future will not always be good. I hope that they will not be deadly. My God is better to me than I am to myself. He allows me to think for myself, have some control over my life, but at times, even when I am out of control, He steps in and takes over. I have to thank Him for stepping in. I have learned when times are bad and even in good times I have to let go and let God. Again, He is the creator and He knows what is best for me if I allow Him to handle the situation at hand. There are times when I think I can do things without Him, how wrong could I be. I need Him in all the things I do, things I say, and where ever I may go. I thirst and crave for more knowledge, but I don't rush to get it like I should, so it is taking me a longer time, but I am moving forward in getting closer and having a better relationship with my God. I know He wants the best for me and He wants to teach me the way in having the best life I can have and to share the same information with others.

TEACH

"to show how or to impart the knowledge."

Teaching is one of the gifts that God gives to us to share with one another. Teaching or being taught is something that happens to us from birth to death. In the beginning of birth, you are taught to eat, hopefully by your parents or by a guardian, how to sit up, how to crawl, how to walk, how to talk and etc. As years passed, you have grown up as young men and women in or out of school, working and maybe supporting a family. In the process of being taught or teaching, you should know about good and bad, right and wrong, as well as who God is and the devil. I have discovered that some parents will teach you about right and wrong, speak on good and bad, but touch on God and the devil, because they weren't exposed to them much when they were growing up. In reality, you should be taught about God and the devil, because they are the main factors that control our everyday living. They are the reasons for our right and wrong behaviors. I try to make living a little simpler and plain; we need to have some balance in our life. Consider these words which are our sources to life.

GOD = POSITIVE = GOOD (to show the balance)

DEVIL = NEGATIVE = EVIL

In life, it's not as simple as it looks. With different people and situations, there are different actions or behaviors. For example:

1. Need food and clothing, but no money, so get a job, or do you rob or steal?

2. Want a new car but not making a lot of money? Do you get a used car until you can afford a new car? Do you make a loan with high car payments with the chance of the car being repossessed?

3. Want to take a trip but no money? Do you run up a credit card, or again wait until you can save enough for the trip?

In all of above, they will cause stress if you aren't taught to make the right decisions or think out your situations carefully. The message that is being shared is that your wants are not your needs and there is a difference. God said to "be anxious for nothing, and keep your mind stayed on Him and He will supply all your needs according to His riches in heaven." He will give you perfect peace. The devil will give all the pain, stress, and suffering you can or cannot handle and more. As you think about the above, remember that the devil is real and that he may cause death.

INHERITANCE

'to receive from ancestors or someone.'

Inheritance is something that is usually left to someone when someone has died. In this case, I am referring to us, everyone on earth. Jesus died for us so that we may have a good life and have it more abundantly. Crazy as it may seem, He left us the earth and everything in it as part of our inheritance and we are supposed to take care of it. Again, are we to take care of it, but are we? Are you doing your part? I have to ask myself the same question at times. Look around and see the trees and the grass dying, animals are being killed on the roads by people, air is being polluted and instead of helping one another, we are killing each other physically and mentally. God has helped me to write this book in hope that we will make a change. I am asking you to search your heart and soul to see where you are and if you are willing to help to make a change.

OBEY

"to follow the commands or guidance of persons' of authority."

Reading this section, you will realize that obeying and having patience are two of the toughest issues in the world to accomplish. The reasons are because we are who we think we are, and most of the times think we know everything and no one can tell us anything. We want what we want now and will do mostly anything to get it right now. The good thing is that my God knows about my shortcomings and is willing to give me a second, third, and even a fourth chance if necessary to get it right. He has a great way of showing me my shortcomings with obedience and patience. The way He shows me is by making me a father with children, then asking me the question, "Do your children know more about life or living then you?" If the answer is no, then do as I asked and obey my request and understand that I know what is best for you and your family. They will also need to understand being patience is very important, because you are going to have to wait on some things. No matter how much you may want something, getting it in a hurry may not be such a good idea, because it may not be right or meant for you at that time.

We need to understand that God's time is not our time, and if we want good and perfect gifts, we must wait on God.

NATURAL

"not artificial, being simple and sincere, or unsophisticated."

This is the reason for a close relationship with my God. My God says come to Him in my natural state, or a state that I may be in, which means drug addict, problem child, prostitute, gay, murder, etc., and He will forgive and help us. Just come simple and sincere. If the truth be told, I don't know of anyone that would accept anybody under those conditions. Forgiving is at times one of the hardest things to do, and it takes time, depending on who it is and what was the offense. I, being a Christian, am supposed to forgive and let go, but again it's hard, and I am not perfect, so I have to pray to do the right thing and obey my God. My God makes me look into my past and see the things I have done and realize that I haven't been that good and someone has overlooked my faults and forgave and even forgot the wrong things that I had committed. So who am I not to do the same? Thank you, Lord.

SUFFICIENT

"adequate to accomplish a purpose or meet a need."

I hope after reading and hopefully understanding this book and what I have tried to accomplish is for you to know the true facts about my God and that He has everything we need to make a change in us so we may help and encourage others in order that we all can unite to make a change in the world. In other words it's not the world that needs to be changed, it's the people in the world. I hope you understand and realize that all the love, money, materialistic things, and spiritual growth you and I would ever need, God has it and He is willing to give it to us. We also need to know that what He has for us should be sufficient and not let greed, selfishness, and wants dominate our self-control or behaviors.

HC

Chapter 8
WISDOM

Worrying

Is

Surely

Downfall

Of

Man

WISDOM

"knowledge, a wise attitude, and good sense of judgment or insight."

Wisdom is something that comes over you when you feel sure that you know what's going on or you have the knowledge of what's happening. It is based on experience.

WORRYING

"to make anxious, upset or a cause of anxiety trouble."

Worrying is one of the tools of the devil to get into your mind and soul. He knows if he can get you to worry about anything, you can't be concentrating on God or anything positive. He knows you won't be at peace but confused and bothered. My God said "if you keep your mind stayed on Him, He will give you perfect peace," but you know that's not what the devil wants you to do. There is a song, "If you pray don't worry, and if you worry don't pray." If you think about it, you have to make that choice whether you want peace or chaos. The choice you make will determine how your day may go and even your life.

IS

"present or being"

The word "is," is a word that again puts the ball or choice in your court or hands. There is a couple of ways to use the word "is." One way to use the word is by using it as a question such as, "What is the weather going to be?" "How is your meal"? The other way is to know something such as, "There is a God." This is the choice you made. You see, no matter how the word is used, it shows that you have made a decision or someone else will be making one. Hopefully, the decisions made have been focused on and thought out carefully. Again, the decision that is made will affect the outcome of your day and your life.

SURELY

"without a doubt."

If you think of this word surely and reading this book, this should mean without a doubt, you do want wisdom in your life. You should always want to know and feel sure of what you are doing and the choices you make are the very best for you and those concerned. If you keep your mind focused on God, He will keep us in perfect peace. You can, without a doubt, be sure that your decisions will be the right ones, even if it may not be what you want. We have to understand that everything we want may not be good for us. Think of the divorce rates and broken homes. We want pretty women, handsome husbands or boyfriends, but if their hearts and souls aren't into a marriage or relationship, than we will be one of the failed relationships. It was our choice and not God's choice.

DOWNFALL

"a sudden fall (as from high rank) or something that causes a downfall."

Downfalls are something we are going to have as long as we live. They only affect us as much as we let them, because they are our choices. I am not going to say that it's easy because it's not, but we can get over it by getting up, which is the key, along with having faith and help from God. The death of a loved one, such as your mother, could really take you for a loop and make you feel that you can't make it, but again you have to believe that God doesn't make mistakes. You may recover in a short time or a long time but it's your choice. If you lose your job or money, you will suffer, but you know you can't stay down long, so you get up and find another job or a way to make the money needed. Downfalls, if they don't kill you, should make you stronger and hopefully much wiser in the way things happen, especially in the way you react and regroup. We have to pray and thank God for experiences, which becomes our testimonies to share with someone else that might be going through some of the same issues.

OF

"a significant background or character element or connected with."

The definition of "of" is a significant element that should relate to you. It's your choice of being part of something positive or negative, even to the point of you allowing people, places, or things to be a significant part of your life. I've found this even in organizations and especially in gangs. Just because you have a title doesn't mean that you are a leader. When you look or think about gangs or organizations, both are a group of individuals, but the differences is the reason they are together. Gangs usually are put together for evil and negative doings, but social or business organizations are together for positive things; so know what you are going to be part of and what your part of the group is.

Man

"male human being or one possessing in high degree the qualities considered distinctive of manhood."

It depends on who we are talking to, in order to get the definition of a man. We already know that Webster's dictionary says man is "the male species of the human beings." We have to determine when that male becomes a man. We know the basic stages, infant, child, boy, teenager, young man, man, or adult, but can we classify every adult male a man or should we say a real man. We all know because you have become of age and can make a baby isn't the characteristic of a man. You could be a boy or a young man. The requirement of a man is to protect, provide and support their family mentally, and physically. My version of a real man, if he does all of the above, is humble and wise enough to know that he can't do all those things sufficiently enough by himself. He knows that he needs faith in God and know that He is going to lead him in the right way for richer or poorer, if he is to stay focused, which is very hard to do when things don't look or feel so prosperous.

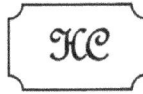

Chapter 9
THANKS

Trustworthy

Heavenly

Anointed

Now

King

Speaks

THANKS

"expression of gratitude"

"Thanks" is saying or giving to someone that has done something for us, and it is our way of showing appreciation in what was done or what has happened.

TRUSTWORTHY

"trusted, assured reliance on the character, strength or truth of someone or something"

When someone or something is classified as being trustworthy, it's a feeling that the person or the thing can be depended upon. You know when you have the feeling of dependability on someone or something, you feel real secure on the project you're working on. A secure feeling is a fueling everyone wants to have, and that is the feeling I have with my God. I know that He has my best interest at heart, and if I let Him help me make my decisions, everything will be all right even if things may not be so good. You know how we get what we want and most of the time it's not what we need, or should have. To give you a few examples: I may buy a new car when I know I can only comfortably afford a used one. I spend my last $125 on a pair of tennis shoes when a pair of $25 tennis shoes will take me the same place and with money left over. I hunger for steak when I only have hot dog money. I know waging and asking my God, He will work things out for me in His time and I will be able to have nice tennis shoes and a steak at times. I realize I need patience and not to be in a hurry, and that's our problem, we don't want to wait. I know that my God is trustworthy and you should feel the same.

HEAVENLY

"a spiritual state of everlasting communication with God, or place of supreme happiness."

We know whether we believe in God and it's a fact that He is above us. I know my God sits high and looks low, looking out for me when I am not looking out for myself. When you are in a near miss accident, in trouble you thought that there was no way out, and money comes from somewhere that you didn't expect, those are experiences of things that happen and not expected, but are granted to us from our heavenly father. When you are in an accident and are not hurt, you go to the store and have money to buy what you want, when you need to go somewhere and you don't have a car, but you can call someone to come and take you to where you have to go, those are other ways our heavenly father shows us His love.

ANOINTED

"consecrate or make or declare sacred."

We claim to hold certain things or people sacred, but not anointed, such as our parents, children, money, cars, husbands, wives, and even homes. We need to understand that these things, even though important to us, are given to us by our Heavenly Father which is anointed and should be sacred to us because of the love He has shown and given us.

NOW

"present time."

"Now" means this very moment. Yesterday has passed and tomorrow is not promised to you. Know if you have not given your life to Christ, now is the time. Now is the time to focus on the things He wants you to do which are good and positive things. My God wants me to be a winner, and I can only do that by thinking and acting in a positive manner. The devil wants us to be his winners, but in reality, we will be losers, because we think and act negatively, and probably causing trouble or some sort of hurt to ourselves, family, or someone else. If you haven't started focusing on good and positive things, now is the time.

KING

"chief among competitors."

My God is the King of my life, as a matter of fact He is the King of everything to me, because He created the earth and everything in it. "Seek ye first the kingdom of God, and everything else will be added to you." In that statement, if you can believe, it shows how powerful and in charge He is. A happy life is what we want, so that means that we need to believe and have patience, because we know that there is going to be some ups and downs, but we aren't in charge. We should be in control of our actions and the way we handle a situation. Again, stay focused on God in good and positive things.

SPEAKS

"to utter words orally or in writing."

My God speaks every day through actions, testimonies, and through the Holy Bible. In the written books of the Bible, He tells us of His life, troubles, death, and resurrection. He tells us and explains the things we will go through, how to handle them, how to live and how to organize our lives so we would be successful and prosperous. God speaks through us by others through our testimonies, which are experiences we face daily, some good and some bad, but we are able to talk and tell others how we made it. Examples:

1. If you were in a car accident and wasn't hurt, someone else died.

2. Being on drugs, I was saved and still here to tell my story, but someone died, in jail, or maybe crippled.

3. I've always had a job so I could work, but someone else, no job, homeless, and stealing or robbing to get something to eat. Think about the testimonies you have and share with others, because through most testimonies, you can help the next person go through easier. The message that we will always hear is to help one another.

Chapter 10
BLESSED

Born Again

Love

Ear

Seasoned

Servant

Eagle

Dwell

BLESSED

"to be consecrated by a religious rite or word, and to invoke divine care."

We need to realize that we are created in a divine care. If you don't believe in God, then figure out how you got here and how your body and your limbs were formed to work together in order to breathe, move, talk, and walk all at the same time. If you are reading this book, you are still alive. When there are so many children, men, and women dying from all kinds of ailments, why are you still here? It is because you are blessed. Realize you are blessed, not because you are so good or perfect but because God has something for you to do. My thought is that since you have been blessed, He wants you to be a blessing to someone else and you can.

BORN-AGAIN

"having experienced a revival of a personal faith or conviction or believer."

Born-again is the flip side of being in the world and the streets. It's a spiritual change that we have to make in order to be a changed person. It's a change from worldly to spiritual beliefs and ways. You are going to be in the world, but not of the world and know the difference. You are now going to ask and have the help and support of God because you are going to be a greater believer. If you are on alcohol or drugs and are truly ready to change, you will get the help you ask for, not necessary instantly, but gradually so you will know there is a change coming slowly, but surely. You will find that you will not go to the same places you use to go, if so not for the same reasons. You will have to experience this change for yourself, not what someone has told you, because of their great feelings, understandings, wisdom, and the peace you will receive, but because you must understand that it takes a lot of work and commitment to get that fulfillment.

LOVE

"strong affection, selfish loyal and benevolent concern for others."

Love is the strongest feeling anyone can have, and believe me that love can conquer all things especially hate. Love is one of the most important L's in life, Live, Love, and Laugh, and if you can do these three things, you will have a happy life. Living happy is a pleasure we all desire, but it's hard to have in the way we may so desire. We must understand that in living, we will have some ups and downs. It's a fact that we all desire ups and no downs, but the fact is we will have downs. Depending on how we handle the downs, it could take us to the point of self-destruction.

Laughter is soothing to the soul and helps us to put some joy in our life. We don't want the kind of laughter where we are making fun or someone is being hurt. Love is a feeling that you never want to give up. You are feeling like you are on cloud nine and getting higher and you don't want to come down. My God is love. One of the reasons for this book is to try to help you understand that God is instilling in us that the love He shares or gives, we are to give and share with others. On that note, we should avoid hating, jealousy, envy, and selfishness. Love accomplishes all that mess, so we can live, love, and laugh, with love being the main factor.

EAR

"the organ for hearing"

Your ears are one of the most important components in communication. God gave us two ears and one mouth so we could listen twice as much as we talk. Being human, we have the bad habit of talking more than we listen. I am learning to listen more, because if I listen before talking, the things I was asking about had already been or being explained. I am not one of those persons that I would say that I heard my God speak to me, but I can say He has His ways of relating to me, sending people or things to show me that He is reaching out to me. He has answered prayers, questions, and situations that were a real concern to me. I am hoping you can feel the same way being I am one of God's messengers, as I share some of my experiences which are my life testimonies. I want to be sent by God to do my part in making a change in your life and hoping that you will do the same for someone else. If you are not listening to what I am saying, you are not using your ears at this moment. You are using another means of communication which are your eyes and mind. You are seeing the cry that we all should be hearing and that is for change and help.

SEASONED

"to make suitable for use occurring at a good or proper time."

Being seasoned is when many of us would like to have been at a younger age. I am now sixty-six years old. I am still working on everything that I am writing about and have been working on them for approximately ten to twelve years. I have several young men and women in my church that are focusing on becoming ordain ministers. It all depends on you being ready to make a change, because tomorrow is not promised to you. If you start now believing and changing in God's sight and become saved, you are on your way to becoming seasoned. Change and seasoned will not happen right away, but it will start.

The change should start in you getting your priorities in order, having a new attitude or a new mindset. I started with the new attitude, then family. We have to look at our families very closely because of the violence and gang activities going on. We need to realize that those children could be ours and let's face the fact that some are our children. We need to make them understand that we weren't born yesterday and we may have not been there when they really needed us, but we are here now wanting to make a change in their lives. We want to be good role models as well as good parents and productive citizens in our communities. We can do our part by praying, asking for help, and believing our God will give it to us. I realize that some of us become seasoned later than others, but it's never too late. If you are a late seasoned person like me, we have to thank God even more because we are still here to share our experiences and give our testimonies. I thank you, God.

SERVANT

"one that serves others."

I know people have a problem being a servant, especially minorities, because of their upbringing and the unfair use of people and not knowing the difference between being a servant and a slave. The difference between being a servant and a slave is that the servant does things because they want to and a slave is made to perform their duties. We think if we serve someone, it's degrading and weak, but it's not, because in God's sight, we are helping someone which is our duty to do. In order to make a change, we have to think differently. Each one helps one. Could you imagine what it would look and feel like, having a lot of love? Think about the times you have helped someone and they gave you something or even said thanks. It should have made you feel good. When someone has helped you with something or you gave them something or said thanks, it's great to see a smile on their face, which will make you feel good. Could you imagine what we could do if we served our communities, families, cities, states, and countries, in showing and sharing the love and commitment God has shown and given to us? The effects could be love and not hatred, unity and not division, joy and not sorrow, but most of all, peace and happiness.

EAGLE

"a large bird of prey."

The eagle is a large bird of prey. My God uses the eagle as an example in the Bible to represent His believers and followers. He wants us to know whose and what we are. If we were eagles, can you imagine what it would be like? We could fly very high, have the best hearing, excellent sight, and very strong, which we would love to have. God knowing His people knows that we get weary, upset, and frustrated when we try to do the things He wants us to do. Trying to be a good servant, respecting people, committing ourselves, communicating, and giving praise is hard when you are trying to give and do these things to people that you feel don't deserve them. God says in the Bible, "They that wait on the Lord shall renew their strength, they shall mount up with wings as eagles, they shall run and not be weary, and they shall walk, and not faint." My interpretation of what God is saying to us is that no matter how hard or long it takes to serve negative people that we don't seem to be getting any head way. We can't give up or get tired of trying to change the situations. God will renew our strength, so we can keep on walking or running to that person or persons no matter where they are and we won't get weary in getting to them. We will not faint or be discouraged after getting to them.

We are conquerors and hopeful a blessing to someone.

DWELLING

"residents, abide, or reside"

Our bodies are really a dwelling place for our organs and spirit. In our body, the three main organs are the brain, the heart, and the spirit. They all work together to make us functional, but the most important organ is the heart. You can function with parts of most organs, but you need the whole heart. You can't live with part of a heart, and that's what God looks at in a person. If your heart is not right, you are not right because that is where the spirit comes into play, whether it's a good or a bad spirit. If your spirit isn't right, it affects the heart which controls what messages are sent to the brain. It determines how you treat or mistreat your fellow man or woman. Try not to let bad spirits dwell within. It's hard to do at times because we do get angry. We hurt and we want to strike out at something or someone. We have to realize when a bad spirit has entered into our heart, we need to stop and pray, asking God to remove that spirit before it causes us to lose our self-control and do some harm. I don't know whether or not you believe in heaven or hell, but you think about your body only being a shell for housing your spirit. So when you die, where do you want your spirit to dwell?

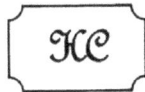

Chapter 11
FOOD FOR THOUGHT!

1. The real key to life is that you have to be ready to do whatever it is you want to do.

2. Remember, in your life, other than God, you are the only person with you, your entire life.

3. Things happen good and bad, so endure, grieve, and move on.

4. Try not to worry about anything, but to pray about everything.

5. Live, Love, Laugh hard and as much as you can.

6. Enjoy simple and small things.

7. Surround yourself with positive things and with people you love.

8. Thank and praise God for everything, good, bad, and indifferent.

9. Respecting others gives you a good feeling in life, or it can cause you to lose your life.

10. Think of the consequences for the choices you make.

Respect   Commit   Change

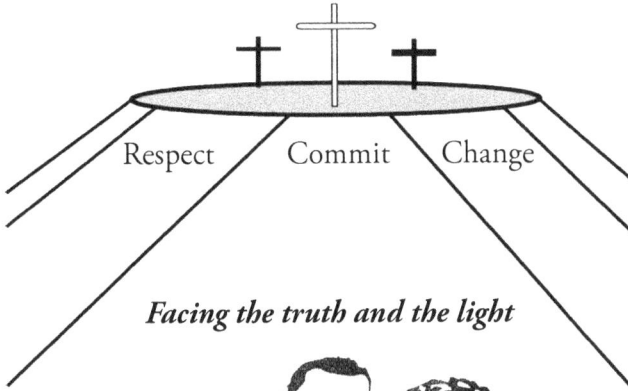

Facing the truth and the light

R E S P E C T

R — ready

E — evaluate

S — self

P — pray

E — expect

C — change

T — time

By
Herman Cooper

ABOUT THE AUTHOR

I thank God for opening my eyes and made me realize that it wasn't all about me. I thank Him for saving me, not only mentally, but physically. I almost died in a car accident, lost good relationships, families, and money. My God showed me a new way to walk and talk. I am not where I would like to be, but I am moving on up in that direction. With my God's help and guidance, I will get there in His time and not mind. I realize that I am nothing without Him and there is nothing without Him, because everything belongs to Him.